OUR CHANGING PLANET

Climate Change

Sarah Harvey

Explore other books at:
WWW.ENGAGEBOOKS.COM

VANCOUVER, B.C.

WWW.ENGAGEBOOKS.COM

Climate Change - Our Changing Planet: *Level 3*
Harvey, Sarah 1955 –
Text © 2023 Engage Books
Design © 2023 Engage Books

Edited by: A.R. Roumanis, Ashley Lee,
Melody Sun & Sarah Harvey
Design by: Mandy Christiansen

Text set in Montserrat Regular.
Chapter headings set in Animated Gothic Light.

FIRST EDITION / FIRST PRINTING

LIBRARY AND ARCHIVES CANADA CATALOGUING IN PUBLICATION

Title: Climate change / Sarah Harvey.
Names: Harvey, Sarah N., 1950- author.
Description: Series statement: Our changing planet

Identifiers: Canadiana (print) 20230447864 | Canadiana (ebook) 2023044787
ISBN 978-1-77476-883-9 (hardcover)
ISBN 978-1-77476-884-6 (softcover)
ISBN 978-1-77476-885-3 (epub)
ISBN 978-1-77476-886-0 (pdf)
ISBN 978-1-77878-122-3 (audio)

Subjects:
LCSH: Climatic changes—Juvenile literature.
LCSH: Global warming—Juvenile literature.
LCSH: Climate change mitigation—Juvenile literature.
LCSH: Global warming—Prevention—Juvenile literature.
LCSH: Nature—Effect of human beings on—Juvenile literature.

Classification: LCC QC903.15 .H37 2023 | DDC J363.738/74—DC23

This project has been made possible in part
by the Government of Canada.

Canada

Contents

What Is Climate Change?

Climate change is a change in weather and temperature that happens over a very long period of time. Earth's climate has changed on its own throughout Earth's history. It can either warm up or cool down.

KEY WORD

Climate: the weather in an area over a long period of time.

Glacial periods are times when Earth is cold and some areas are covered in ice. Interglacial periods are times when Earth is warmer and ice from glacial periods melts. Earth is currently in an interglacial period.

The last glacial period ended about 11,700 years ago.

A Closer Look

This is the first climate change caused by humans. Earth is now warming up faster than it ever has in human history. Earth is about 1.8° Fahrenheit (1° Celsius) warmer than it was in 1760.

A few degrees may not seem like a lot, but it can make a big difference. Sea turtles lay eggs in the sand. If the sand is 88°F (31.1°C), female turtles will hatch. If the sand is 82°F (27.8°C), male turtles will hatch. Both male and female turtles are needed to make more turtles.

Scientists think the temperature could go up another 3.6°F (2°C) by 2100.

What Are Greenhouse Gases?

Earth is covered by a blanket of gas called an atmosphere. Some of the gases in the atmosphere trap heat from the Sun and cause temperatures to rise. These are called greenhouse gases.

The main greenhouse gases causing climate change are carbon dioxide and methane.

Many greenhouse gases enter the atmosphere when fossil fuels are burned. Fossil fuels are things like gas, oil, and coal. They come from living things that died millions of years ago.

Human Caused Climate Change

Fossil fuels are often burned to make energy. Energy makes things like lights, TVs, and cars work. In 2019, about 84 percent of all energy came from burning fossil fuels.

Farming also creates greenhouse gases. Animals like cows, pigs, and sheep let out methane when they burp. About 32 percent of all methane created by human activities comes from farming.

The Changing Weather

Climate change causes weather all over the world to change. Big storms happen more often. These storms can lead to floods. Strong winds damage homes and other buildings.

The number of known natural disasters around the world went up from 406 in 2021 to 421 in 2022.

There are more hot days now than there were in the past. Hot days can lead to **droughts**. If forests become too dry, fires spread fast. They are a danger to both people and animals.

KEY WORD

Droughts: long periods without rain.

Effects on the Planet

Climate change is causing oceans to get warmer. This heat causes **coral reefs** to become sick and sometimes die. The sea life that once lived around coral reefs no longer has a place to live.

KEY WORD

Coral reefs: places in the ocean where lots of sea life lives.

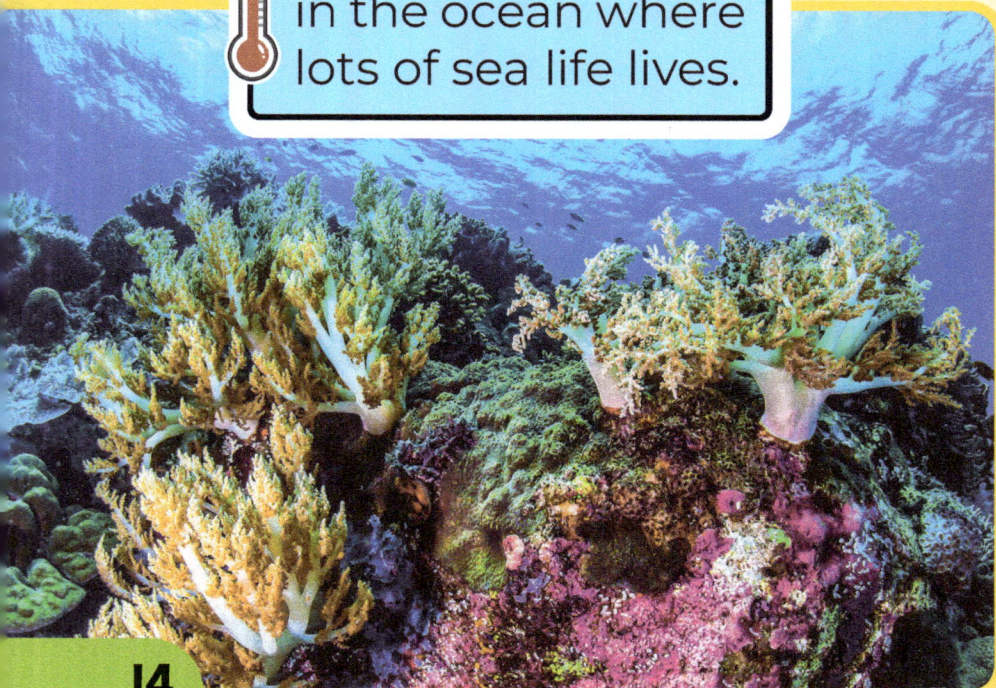

Warmer weather also makes sea ice melt. Sea ice is important to many animals. Polar bears need to go onto sea ice to catch seals to eat. If sea ice melts, polar bears have trouble finding enough food.

The Arctic loses about 13 percent of its sea ice every ten years.

Effects on Humans

Weather changes can make life much harder for poor people. Water is harder to find. Food can be harder to grow.

Every year, about 20 million people have to leave their homes because of extreme weather events.

Climate change can also affect people's health. Smoke from fires can make it hard for some people to breathe. People can become sick if the weather gets too hot. Bad storms can cause injuries or death.

Climate Change Around the World 1

The Maldives is a country in the Indian Ocean that is made up of small islands. These islands are getting smaller as sea levels rise. They may soon be completely covered with water.

When Glacier National Park in the United States opened in 1910, it had about 150 glaciers. Rising temperatures have caused many of these to melt. In 2015, there were fewer than 30 glaciers left.

Climate Change Around the World 2

Climate change is causing long droughts in Madagascar. There is not enough water to keep people, animals, and plants alive. When plants die, people and animals also have less to eat.

Madagascar is home to many plants and animals that cannot be found anywhere else in the world.

The Great Barrier Reef in Australia is the biggest coral reef in the world. Warming oceans are not the only thing putting it in danger. Climate change is causing more **cyclones**. These cyclones can cause parts of the reef to break.

KEY WORD

Cyclones: large storms made up of strong winds and rain that spin in a circle.

Climate Change Solutions 1

Countries around the world are starting to use renewable energy. This is energy that comes from something that cannot be used up, like wind or sunlight. Solar panels are used to make energy from the Sun and windmills are used to make energy from the wind.

Many cars work by burning gas. This means they are making carbon dioxide that goes into the air. More and more people are buying electric cars. They run on a battery that can be recharged, just like a tablet or a cell phone. They do not make carbon dioxide.

It is possible for airplanes to fly around the world using only energy from the Sun.

Climate Change Solutions 2

Trees soak up carbon dioxide. People all over the world are planting trees to replace the ones that have been cut down. This helps keep Earth from warming up faster.

Most of the things people use in their everyday lives are made in **factories**. Factories create a lot of greenhouse gases. People are making sure to take care of the things they have so they last longer. They do not need to buy as much and factories do not need to make as much.

Factories: places where machines are used to make things people can buy.

The Helpers

Greta Thunberg is an environmental activist. This means she works to protect Earth. Since she was 15, she has been telling world leaders they are not doing enough to stop climate change.

David Suzuki is a scientist who started the David Suzuki Foundation. He and his foundation study climate change and come up with ways to stop it. They are working to help Canada use only renewable energy by 2050.

How Can You Help?

Try to use less energy in your home. Turn off the lights when you are not in the room. Turn off computers, tablets, or video games when you are not using them.

Start your own fruit and vegetable garden! The food we buy often travels from far away on boats or in cars. These boats and cars burn fossil fuels. Growing your own food makes the trip to your table shorter.

Quiz

Test your knowledge of climate change by answering the following questions. The questions are based on what you have read in this book. The answers are listed on the bottom of the next page.

1 What is climate change?

2 Is Earth warming up faster than it ever has in human history?

3 What are the main greenhouse gases causing climate change?

4 What are droughts?

5 How many people have to leave their homes every year because of bad weather events?

6 What is renewable energy?

Explore Other Level 3 Readers.

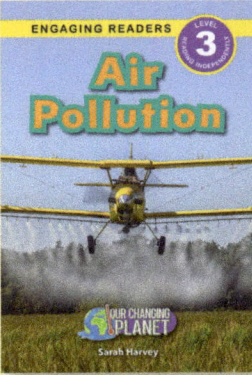

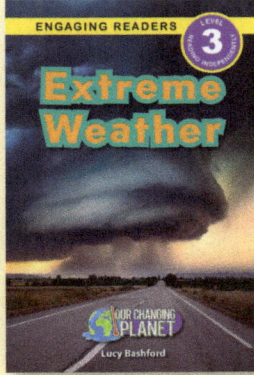

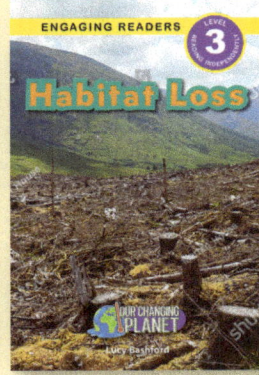

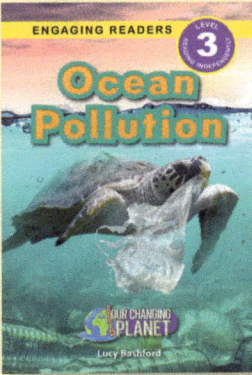

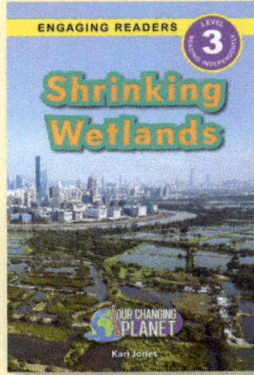

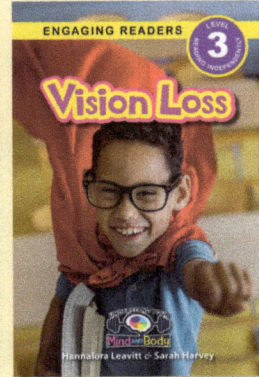

ENGAGING READERS — LEVEL 3
Air Pollution
OUR CHANGING PLANET
Sarah Harvey

ENGAGING READERS — LEVEL 3
Extreme Weather
OUR CHANGING PLANET
Lucy Bashford

ENGAGING READERS — LEVEL 3
Habitat Loss
OUR CHANGING PLANET
Lucy Bashford

ENGAGING READERS — LEVEL 3
Ocean Pollution
OUR CHANGING PLANET
Lucy Bashford

ENGAGING READERS — LEVEL 3
Shrinking Wetlands
OUR CHANGING PLANET
Kari Jones

ENGAGING READERS — LEVEL 3
Diabetes
Mind and Body
Kit Caudron-Robinson

ENGAGING READERS — LEVEL 3
Obesity
Mind and Body
Kit Caudron-Robinson

ENGAGING READERS — LEVEL 3
Autism
Mind and Body
AJ Knight

ENGAGING READERS — LEVEL 3
Vision Loss
Mind and Body
Hannalora Leavitt & Sarah Harvey

Visit www.engagebooks.com/readers

Answers:
1. A change in weather and temperature that happens over a very long period of time 2. Yes 3. Carbon dioxide and methane 4. Long periods without rain 5. About 20 million 6. Energy that comes from something that cannot be used up